CONTENTS

20
HURRICANE LAMP CENTERPIECE

22
BIRDCAGE WREATH

24
DOE & FAWN WREATH

26
RED MAGNOLIA WREATH

28
BIRDHOUSE WREATH

30
ROCKING HORSE WREATH

32
WHITE LILY WREATH

Original projects designed by
Carole McCoy

© 1993 Mark Publishing
Graphic Design: Barry Geller
Photography: Todd Tsukushi
Stylist: Nan Geller

A special thanks for props to Smith China in Santa Cruz, CA and "From the Heart" in Aptos, CA.

Materials & models supplied by Wang's International, Inc., Memphis, TN

PRINTED IN HONG KONG

One

Making Bows

Materials

- *Ribbon*
- *Floral Wire*

FLORIST BOW

1 Cut a length of ribbon twice the streamer length (for one set of streamers).

FOR 6" STREAMERS CUT A 12" LENGTH OF RIBBON

2 Form a loop with the remaining ribbon and hold between thumb and index finger.

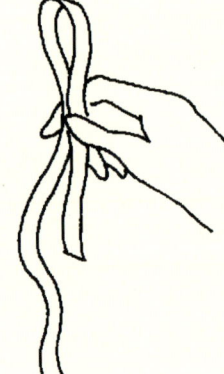

3 Continue forming loops in each direction.

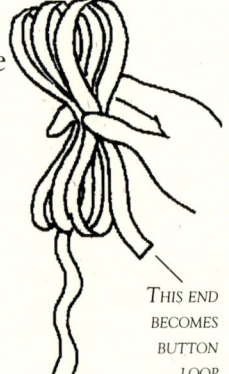

THIS END BECOMES BUTTON LOOP

4 Before securing bow center with wire, add button loop to top by twisting the end of the tail on top of the bow (making sure the right side is out) over and under your thumb.

5 Place wire through the small center loop (button loop) and twist in back of bow.

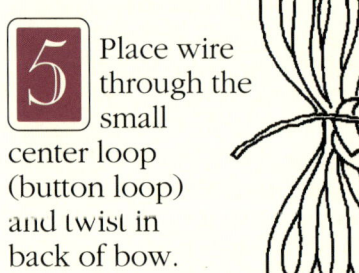

6 Fan out the loops to make a full bow. To add the streamers, thread through loop and tie in back of bow. Repeat for as many streamers as desired.

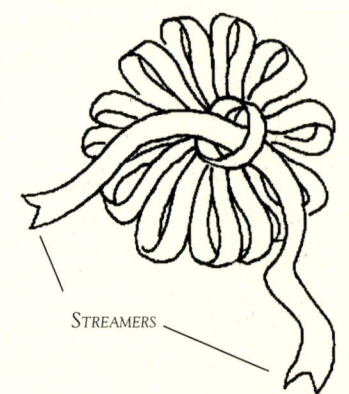

STREAMERS

LOOPY BOW

1 Make a loop leaving streamer the desired length.

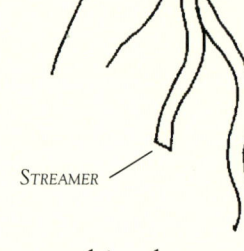

STREAMER

2 Continue making loops keeping them uniform in size until bow is full and enough ribbon is left over to make remaining streamer.

3 Secure center of bow with wire and fan out.

Two

Jingle Bell Doorpiece

Materials:

- 1 - 24" Angel Pine Swag
- 7 - 2 3/4" Gold Liberty Bells
- 7 - Gold Glittered Poinsettia with Berry Picks
- 2 - 18" Gold Plated Holly Sprays
- 6 1/4 Yards - 2" Red Mylar Velvet Ribbon
- 1 Pkg. - Green Packaged Floral Wire
- 1 Pkg. - Gold Glittered Birch Sticks
- Glue (hot glue recommended)

Instructions:

1 Use entire length of ribbon to make 12" florist bow with streamers of 10". Fasten with floral wire and attach to center of swag.

2 Fill in both above and below bow with gold glittered birch sticks, gold plated holly sprays, gold glitter poinsettia/berry picks and gold Liberty bells. Glue all securely in place. Thread some wire through brangh in back to hang.

Three

Nutcracker Wreath

Materials:

- 1 - 30" Frosted Colorado Pine Wreath
- 1 - 20" Nutcracker Doll
- 1 - 4 1/4" Wood Rocking Horse
- 2 - 4" Gold Plated Musical Notes
- 2 - 5" Gold Shiny Musical Instruments
- 1 - 3 1/2" Wood Toy Soldier Ornament
- 4 - 3" Flocked Santas
- 2 - 6" Paper Santa Elves
- 8 - 4" Plastic Candy Cane Ornaments
- 4 - 2 1/2" Pom Pon Characters
- 1 - 4" Plastic Santa Ornament
- 3 - Wood Christmas Ornaments
- 4 Stems - 18" White Plated Holly Spray
- 1 - Red Poinsettia Bush
- 7 Stems - Red Bridal Wreath
- 1 - 9' Gold Metallic Note Garland
- 6 Yards - Christmas Poinsettia Paper Ribbon
- 1 Pkg. - Green Packaged Floral Wire
- Glue (hot glue recommended)

Instructions:

1 Untwist paper ribbon. Make a 16" florist bow with 17" streamers.

2 Attach bow to bottom of wreath, just right of center, with glue and floral wire. See photograph for placement.

3 Glue nutcracker above bow on right side of wreath.

4 Separate iridescent holly into small sprays. Glue around wreath.

5 Arrange various ornaments, including candy canes, Santa Claus assortment, musical ornaments, snowman, rocking horse, etc., around wreath as desired. Glue in place.

6 Fill in with red bridal wreath and poinsettia blooms.

7 Loop and drape metallic musical note garland on wreath, spot-gluing in place.

Optional: Place a small Santa Teddy inside wreath after hanging

Magical Santa

Materials:

- 1 - 30" Frosted Colorado Pine Wreath
- 1 - 16" White Fabric Santa
- 2 Stems - 20" White Plated Cedar Spray
- 8 - Iced Silver Berry Clusters
- 4 Pkgs. - 4 1/2" Mica Plastic Icicles
- 6 Pkgs. - 1 1/4" Gold Plastic Star Ornaments
- 2 Yards - Gold Metallic Thread
- 34 Segments - 9' White w/Glitter Plastic Snowflake Garland
- 1 Pkg. - 9' Gold Star Wire Garland
- 1 Pkg. - 9' Iridescent Plastic Bead Garland
- 5 Yards - 36 Piece Iridescent Wire Metallic Ribbon
- 1 Pkg. - Green Packaged Floral Wire
- 1 Pkg. - Gold Glittered Birch Sticks
- 1 Pkg. - Dried Corkscrew Sticks
- Glue (hot glue recomended)

Instructions:

1 Attach white Santa to bottom of wreath with floral wire. Also, glue where needed.

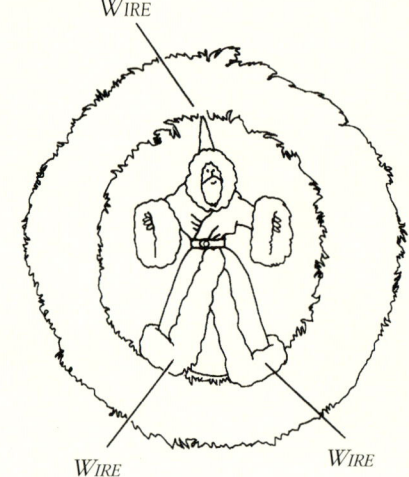

2 Using iridescent wired ribbon make two 9" florist bows with streamers. Glue one on each side of wreath beside Santa.

3 Drape and twist a length of ribbon on left side of wreath beginning at top of wreath and ending at top of bow.

4 Separate white sprays into sections. Glue sections around bows as shown in photo. Add glittered birch sticks, icicles and snowflakes cut from garland.

5 Glue grape clusters in center of bows and above bows. Drape bead garland from one bow to the other. Glue to secure.

6 Loop gold star garland around wreath, spot-gluing in place.

7 Embellish Santa's robe with icicles, stars and snowflakes. Glue.

Seven

Doves and Cherubs

Materials:

- 1 - 14" Natural Birch Wreath
- 1 - 12" Natural Birch Wreath
- 1 - 7" Flying White Dove
- 3 - 4" White Feather Cotton Doves
- 3 - 3 1/2" Iridescent Plastic Cherubs
- 4 Stems - 18" Gold Plated Holly Spray
- 12 Stems - White Bridal Wreath
- 6 Pieces - 20" Green Plated Cedar Spray
- 1 Stem - Eucalyptus
- 12 - Red Glitter Poinsettia Berry Picks
- 12 - Raspberry Cone Picks
- 12 Yards - Red/Green Striped Ribbon
- 1 Piece - Green Packaged Floral Wire
- Small Amount - Gold Dried Gyp
- 1 Pkg. - Gold Glittered Birch Sticks
- Glue (hot glue recommended)

Instructions:

1 Place 12" wreath inside 14" wreath forming a cross at top and bottom.

2 Make one small arrangement for inside of ball and one larger arrangement for top, using the following items: cedar sprays, holly sprays, bridal wreath, poinsettias, raspberry cone picks, glittered birch sticks and gold holly leaves. Arrange as desired or refer to photograph. Attach to wreath with glue or floral wire as needed.

3 Using velvet ribbon, make two loopy bows, one 11" for bottom of ball and one 9" for top of ball. Add 4 streamers to each bow and glue in place.

4 Place one dove on top of bow and two inside ball. Glue to secure. Add cherubs as desired.

Eight

Nine

Musical Wreaths

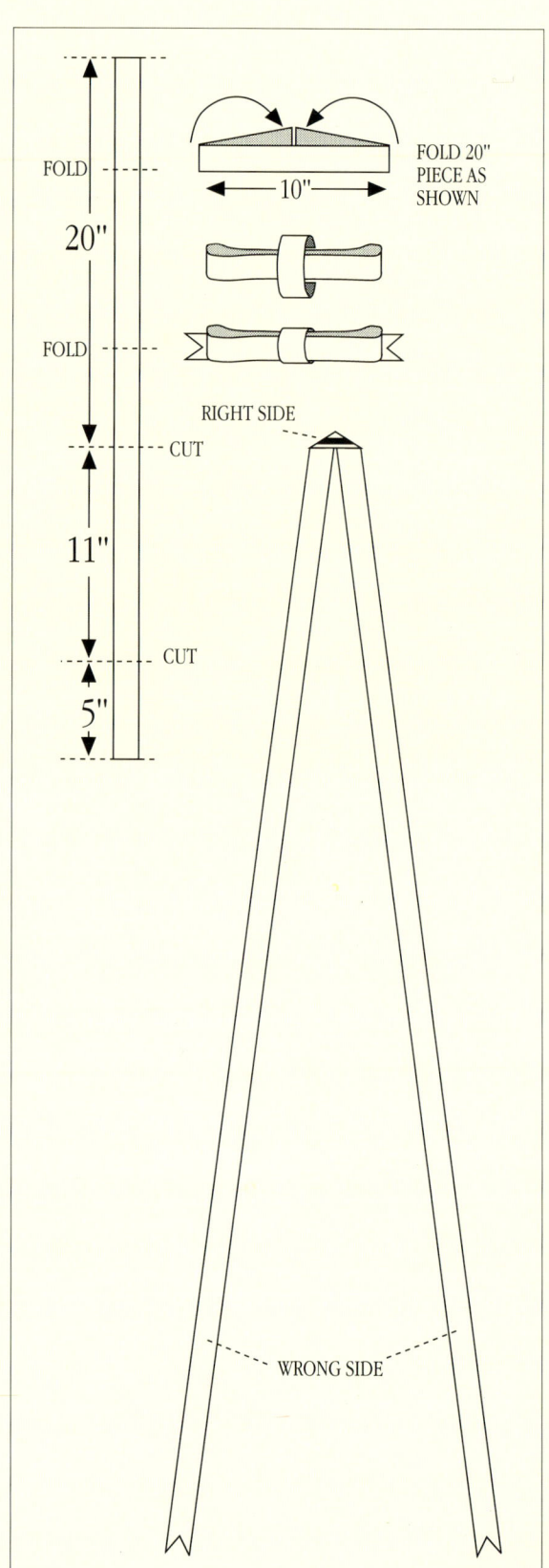

FOLD
20"
FOLD
CUT
11"
CUT
5"

10"
FOLD 20" PIECE AS SHOWN

RIGHT SIDE

WRONG SIDE

Ten

Materials:

- 1 - 10" Small Lacquered Rattan Wreath
- 1 - Canadian Pine Pick
- 1 - 3 1/2" Brass French Horn
- 1 - 3" Wood Harp
- 1 - 5 1/2" Gold Metal Musical Staff
- 2 - 3" Paper Music Scrolls
- 1 Stem - Holly Berry Spike
- 1 1/2 Yards - 9' Gold Metallic Note Garland
- 2 3/4 Yards - Red/Green Mylar Velvet Ribbon
- Small Amount - 10" Grapevine Wreath *
- Small Amount - 14" Green Packaged Floral Wire *
- 4 Yards - Red/Green Mylar Velvet Ribbon **
- Glue (hot glue recommended)

* A onetime purchase of this product will yield enough material for each project in this collection.

** Extra Ribbon is intended for use in display of this collection

HANGING RIBBON

1. Cut one yard of ribbon and section into pieces of 20", 11" and 5" in length.

2. Fold ends of 20" piece to meet at center back. Fold 5" piece over center of 20" piece and glue at back. Glue bow to 11" piece of ribbon, with cuts made in ends.

3. Glue completed bow to remaining three yards of ribbon which have been folded as shown in diagram.

SMALL GRAPEVINE MUSICAL WREATH

Instructions:

1 Attach sections of Canadian pine pick to top of wreath pointing in all directions. Secure with glue.

2 Make 7" loopy bow with 4 1/2" streamers and place in center of pine arrangement with floral wire.

3 Cut sections of grapevine wreath and gold metallic note garland to add to arrangement. Glue or wire to secure.

4 Using glue, add holly berry spike pieces, wood harp, brass French horn, metal music staff and paper music scrolls as desired. Refer to photograph for placement ideas.

Musical Wreaths

Medium Grapevine Musical Wreath

Materials:

- 1 - 14" Medium Lacquered Rattan Wreath
- 1 1/2 - Canadian Pine Pick
- 1 - 7" Brass French Horn
- 1 - 6" Wood Violin
- 1 - 5 1/2" Gold Metal Musical Staff
- 3 - 3" Paper Music Scrolls
- 2 1/2 Stems - Holly Berry Spikes
- 2 Yards - 9' Gold Metallic Note Garland
- 1 1/2 Yards - Red/Green Mylar Velvet Ribbon
- Small Amount - 10" Grapevine Wreath *
- Small Amount - 14" Green Packaged Floral Wire *
- Glue (hot glue recommended)

Instructions:

1 Glue sections of Canadian pine pick to wreath at ten o'clock position and a small amount at three o'clock position.

2 Using 1 1/2 yards ribbon, make a 9" loopy bow with 5" streamers. Attach to wreath, over larger pine arrangement, using floral wire.

3 Untwist grapevine wreath and cut sections to add to arrangement. Secure among greenery using glue or floral wire. Repeat with two yards of gold metallic note garland.

4 Add pieces of holly berry spike, wooden violin, brass French horn, metal music staff and paper scrolls using glue to fasten firmly. Refer to photograph for placement ideas.

Twelve

LARGE GRAPEVINE MUSICAL WREATH

Materials:

- 1 - 20" Large Lacquered Rattan Wreath
- 2 - Canadian Pine Picks
- 1 - 14" Brass French Horn
- 1 - 8 3/4" Wood Violin
- 3 - 5 1/2" Gold Metal Musical Staffs
- 4 - 3" Paper Music Scrolls
- 6 - Holly Berry Spikes
- 3 1/2 Yards - 9' Gold Metallic Note Garland
- 3 Yards - Red/Green Mylar Velvet Ribbon
- Small Amount - 10" Grapevine Wreath *
- Small Amount - 14" Green Packaged Floral Wire *
- Glue (hot glue recommended)

Instructions:

1 Using glue, attach sections of Canadian pine pick to bottom half of wreath.

2 Make a 12" loopy bow using three yards of mylar velvet ribbon. Leave 9" streamers to dangle. Attach to bottom center of wreath with floral wire.

3 Cut sections of untwisted grapevine wreath. Glue or wire grapevine sections and metallic note garland in greenery as desired.

4 Use glue to attach brass French horn, paper music scrolls, wooden violin, pieces of holly berry spike and metal music staffs. See photograph for placement.

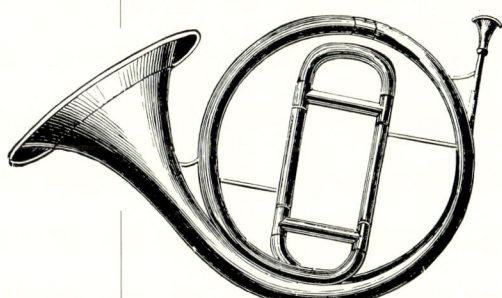

Thirteen

Wild Deer Wreath

Materials:

- 1 - 18" Round, Unwrapped Straw Wreath
- 1 - 9" Flocked Deer With Antlers
- 2 Sprays - Douglas Fir Spray
- 4 Stems - Harvest Pick
- 5 Stems - Fall Nut Spray
- 3 Stems - Apricot/Flame Dried-Look Statice
- 6 - 18" Pheasant Tail Feathers
- 2 Pkg. - 32" Cattails
- 1 Pkg. - Natural Raffia
- Small Amount - 14" Grapevine Wreath
- Small Amount - Spanish Moss
- 1 Pkg. - Green Packaged Floral Wire
- 6 Yards - 1 1/2" Natural Sinamay Ribbon
- 3 - Sponge Mushrooms
- 5 - Pine Cones
- Glue (hot glue recommended)

Instructions:

1 Glue deer in center of straw wreath. Place greenery around deer, extending in all directions.

2 Make an 8" loopy bow with natural sinamay ribbon, glue in place under deer. Add four harvest picks around bow. Place berry sprays around picks and add statice.

3 Place pheasant feathers on each side of wreath, pointing outward to left and right. Secure ends in greenery.

4 Tie a bundle of cattails together, 3 to 5 on each end, and glue securely beneath bow and picks. See drawing at left.

5 Make raffia puffs by folding raffia in half to form loops. Wire ends to secure and place throughout wreath.

6 Attach sponge mushrooms, one behind front legs of deer, one below bow and one to right of bow near hind legs of deer.

7 Add pine cones as desired.

8 Pull apart grapevine wreath and wire ends of selected segments into greenery creating large loops. Refer to photograph for help with placement.

Fifteen

Victorian Half Tree

Materials:

- 1 - 2 1/2' Canadian Pine Tree
- 6 - 4" White Medallion Doilies
- 6 - 3" White Plastic Baskets
- 3 Pkgs. - 1 3/4" Sisal Wreaths
- 3 Pkgs. - 3/4" Iridescent Plastic Snowflakes
- 10 - Fall Fruit/Cone Picks
- 16 - 1" Burgundy Dried Rosebuds
- 32 - 1" Mauve Dried Open Roses
- Small Amount - Bleached Gyp
- 2 1/4 Yards - 3mm White Pearl Garland
- 2 3/4 Yards - 3/4" White Ruffled Poly Cluny
- 2 1/2 Yards - 1/8" White Woven Edge Satin Ribbon
- 10 Yards - 1/8" Burgundy Woven Edge Satin Ribbon
- 9 Yards - 1/8" Mauve Woven Edge Satin Ribbon
- 1 1/4 Yards - 1 1/2" Mauve Moire Ribbon
- Small Amount - White Ceramcoat Paint Squeeze Bottle
- Small Amount - Glorious Metallic Gold DecoArt Americana Paint
- Glue (hot glue recommended)

Instructions:

1 Paint tree basket white and dry-brush with gold paint. Using mauve moire ribbon make large, flat bow and glue securely to top of basket, just below bottom boughs of tree.

2 Very lightly dry-brush each plastic basket with gold paint. Using hot glue, trim upper edge of baskets with sections of ruffled cluny, then glue pearl garland over basket handles and at base of baskets. Cut six 7" sections of 1/8" burgundy ribbon, tie 1 1/4" bows and glue to base of handles on one side of plastic baskets. Fill each basket with color combination of six roses and small amount of bleached gyp. Tie baskets to tree branches using six 12" sections of burgundy ribbon.

3 Fold doilies in half creating fans. Thread three doilies with 7" sections of mauve ribbon and three with 7" sections of burgundy ribbon. Between two rows of threaded ribbon, glue 4" segments of pearl garland. Cut six 12" sections each of mauve, white and burgundy 1/8" ribbon. Use combination of three colors to tie bows, then glue to bottom center of fans. Tie fans to tree branches with 12" sections of mauve ribbon, making simple bows.

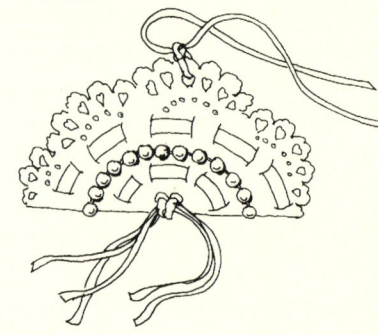

4 Remove red bows from sisal wreaths and replace with mauve bows made of 12" sections of ribbon. Over center of each bow, glue one mauve rose and small amount of bleached gyp. Tie wreaths to tree branches with 10" sections of mauve ribbon.

5 Dry-brush approximately ten snowflakes with hint of gold. Attach to tree with simple bows of burgundy ribbon.

6 Glue fruit/cone picks and small amounts of bleached gyp throughout tree to fill in.

Seventeen

CHRISTMAS TOPIARY

Materials:

- 1 - 12" PVC Topiary Tree
- 1 - 8" Wild Rattan Wreath
- 1 Stem - 18" Gold Plated Holly Spray
- 1/3 Bush - Glacier Ivy
- 4 Stems - Red Glitter Bridal Wreath
- 5 Bunches - 1" Red Dried Rosebud
- 2 - 2" Red Cardinals
- 1 - 1" Cardinal On Nest
- Small Amount - Spanish Moss
- 4 Yards - 4mm Gold Wire Mylar Ribbon
- 1 Pkg. - Mini Lotus Pods
- Glue (hot glue recommended)

Instructions:

1 Place tree inside center of wreath and carefully glue together at front.

2 Begin by gluing ivy on top of wreath creating semi-circle, and on top of each ball segment of tree.

3 Fill in as desired with gold plated holly, red bridal wreath, dried rosebuds, mini lotus pods and Spanish moss. Place Spanish moss at base of tree also. Glue each piece securely.

4 Place one cardinal on each level.

5 Glue 4" loopy mylar bow beneath first ball segment and 4" loopy mylar bow with dried rose center beneath second ball segment. See photograph.

6 Add twists of mylar ribbon to each level of arrangement, if desired.

Sunburst Centerpiece

Materials:

- 1 - Large Gold Sunburst Wreath
- 1 - 5"x 6" Red 3-Wick Candle
- 8 Stems - Canadian Pine Spray
- 1 Stem - 18" Gold Plated Holly Spray
- 1 1/2 Stems - 18" Green Plated Holly Spray
- 9 Stems - Della Robbia Harvest Pick
- 1 Roll - Red/Green/Gold Mylar Twisted Ribbon
- 1 - 8"x 1" Styrofoam Disc OR 1 - 2"X 12"X 36" Foam Sheet
- 1 Pkg. - 14" Green Floral Wire

Instructions:

1 Place foam disc, 8" in diameter and 1" thick (either pre-cut package or cut from styrofoam sheet) in center of glittered birch stick sunburst. Set candle on foam disc in center.

2 Begin filling in around candle with green holly spray, Canadian pine stems and gold plated holly. Refer to photograph for placement of items.

3 Use Della Robbia to fill in closest to candle.

4 Cut sections of mylar twisted ribbon in 15" lengths. Loop and secure with floral wire. Punch ribbon loops into foam disc as desired.

Note: Ornaments shown in photo are optional.

Hurricane Lamp Centerpiece

Materials:

- 10 Stems - 16" Angel Pine Spray
- 1 Bush - Pink Marble Natural Poinsettia Bush
- 7 Stems - 10mm Frosted Mauve Berry Spray
- 5 Yards - 1 1/2" Mauve Sinamay Ribbon
- 1 Block - 12" x 12" x 2" Desert Dry Floral Foam
- 1 - 3"x 6" Pink Candle
- 1 - 4 3/4"x 11 5/8" Glass Hurricane Lamp

Instructions:

1 Cut two pieces of floral foam, one 5"x 4"x 2" and one 3 1/4"x 4"x 2". Round corners of smaller piece to fit inside base of hurricane lamp then glue to top of larger piece.

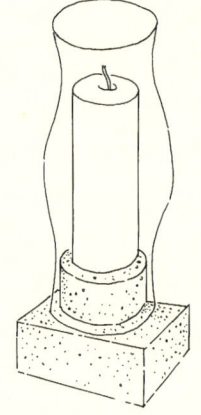

2 Add candle, gluing to secure, to top of foam blocks and add Spanish moss around base of candle and sides of block to hide foam. Place hurricane lamp over candle and moss as shown.

3 Place stems of pine sprays into large foam block to create wreath-like circle around lamp.

4 Using sinamay ribbon, make two 9" loopy bows and place one bow on each side of hurricane lamp. Add separate ribbon loops between bows.

5 Arrange poinsettia and berry stems around base of hurricane lamp, filling in pine sprays. Refer to photograph.

Twenty one

Birdcage Wreath

Materials:

- 1 - 24" Natural Grapevine Wreath
- 1 - 8" Brass Plate Birdcage of Wire
- 4 - 1 1/2" Wine Cardinals
- 5 - 6" Burgundy Glitter Poinsettias
- 2 Stems - 18" Gold Plated Holly Spray
- 7 - 2" Burgundy Dried Pear Picks
- 4 - 7" Purple Poly Foam Grape Clusters
- Small Amount - Spanish Moss
- 1 Block - 8"x 4"x 3" Desert Dry Floral Foam
- 1 Wire - 14" Green Packaged Floral Wire
- 1 Pkg. - Dried Cedar Spray
- 1 Pkg. - Gold Glittered Birch Sticks
- Glue (hot glue recommended)

Instructions:

Wreath

1. At top of wreath, to left of center, glue bits of cedar spray, gold plated holly, gold glittered birch sticks and Spanish moss. Nest one cardinal in center of spray. Cut small section from grape cluster and secure beneath cardinal.

2. At bottom of wreath, right of center, begin by gluing down cedar spray with majority at three o'clock and seven o'clock. Next add gold plated holly and glittered birch sticks. At five o'clock on wreath add three grape clusters. Fill in with Spanish moss and pear picks. Nest cardinal in center of arrangement, securing with glue. Refer to photograph for placement of items.

Birdcage

1. Cut 1/4 of foam block and place in bottom of cage, concealing with Spanish moss.

2. Arrange sprays of dried cedar and gold plated holly between bars of cage and attach by placing stems into foam block.

3. Place one grape cluster in bottom front of cage. Glue in place. Refer to photograph.

4. Nest one cardinal and one pear pick inside cage.

5. Place one cardinal on top of cage on bed of cedar, gold plated holly and Spanish moss. See photograph.

6. Using floral wire hang cage from top center of wreath.

Twenty two

Twenty three

Doe & Fawn Wreath

Materials:

- 1 - 20" Canadian Pine Wreath
- 1 - 4 3/4" x 3 1/2" Flocked Doe with Fawn
- 9 - Gold Glitter Poinsettia with Berries Picks
- 3 - 14" Pheasant Feathers
- 3 - 12" Cinnamon Sticks
- Small Amount - Stardust Gyp
- Small Amount - Spanish Moss
- 1/3 Block - 8"x 3"x 4" Desert Dry Foam
- 1 Pkg. Gold Glittered Birch Sticks
- 1 - Dried Pod
- 2 - Mini Lotus Pods
- Small Amount - Preserved Cedar Sprays
- 1 - 31" Circumference Fishbowl, 8" Tall with 5 1/2" Opening
- Glue (hot glue recommended)

Instructions:

Bowl

1 Cut piece of foam to fit in the bottom of bowl. Place doe with fawn on top of foam. Glue in place. Add Spanish moss around edges of foam.

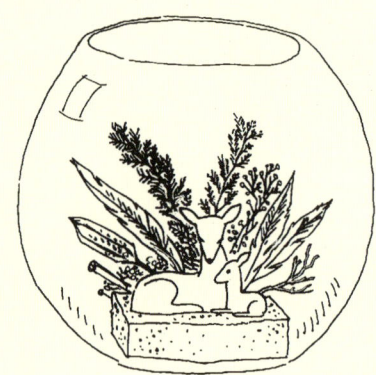

2 Place feathers, cedar sprays and dried pod behind deer. Arrange remaining pods, gold birch sticks, cinnamon sticks and gyp around deer as shown.

Wreath

3 Glue gold poinsettia/berry picks on one half of wreath as shown. Fill in with gold birch sticks.

4 Place bowl in center of wreath for a tablepiece.

Twenty five

Red Magnolia Wreath

Materials:

- 1 - 24" Grapevine Wreath
- 3 Stems - Red Grand Magnolia
- 1 Pkg. - Green Eucalyptus
- Small Amount - Spanish Moss
- 2 Yards - Gold Wire Metallic Ribbon
- 1 Pkg. - Green Packaged Floral Wire
- 1 Pkg. Gold Glittered Birch Sticks
- 6 Stems - 12" Lotus Pods
- 1 Pkg. - Preserved Cedar Sprays
- Glue (hot glue recommended)

Instructions:

1 Place cedar sprays, eucalyptus and gold birch sticks across bottom of wreath with ends facing each other. Glue in place.

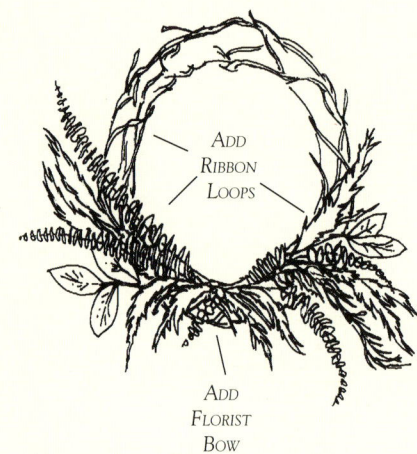

Add Ribbon Loops

Add Florist Bow

2 Using gold metallic ribbon make an 11" florist bow with streamers. Glue bow on greenery.

3 Make three ribbon loops by folding over ribbon and securing with wire. Place these in arrangement as shown in drawing.

4 Arrange magnolias and lotus pods referring to photograph for placement. Glue to secure.

5 Fill in with Spanish moss.

Twenty six

Twenty-seven

Birdhouse Wreath

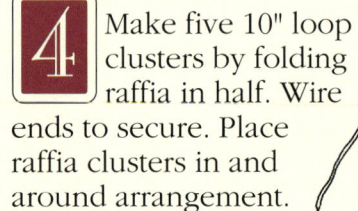

Materials:

- 1 - 18" Round, Unwrapped Straw Wreath
- 1 - Bamboo Birdhouse
- 1 - 2 1/2" Birdhouse Pick
- 4 - 1 1/4" Rust Sparrows
- 1 1/2 Stems - Canadian Pine Spray
- 2 Stems - Flame Dried-Look Statice
- 5 Stems - Fall Nut Spray
- 4 - Harvest Picks
- Small Amount - Natural Raffia
- Small Amount - Spanish Moss
- 3 1/4 Yards - 1 1/2" Natural Sinamay Ribbon
- 1 Pkg. - Green Packaged Floral Wire
- Small Amount - Preserved Cedar
- Glue (hot glue recommended)

Instructions:

1 Glue larger birdhouse at bottom of wreath. Place Spanish moss around house.

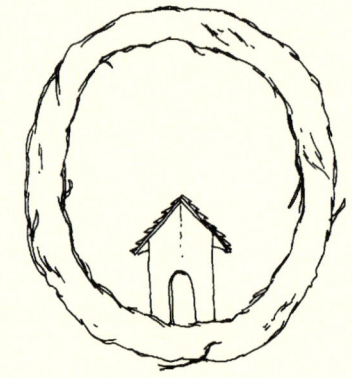

2 Arrange stems of fall nut spray and Canadian pine spray across bottom of wreath. Glue or wire into place.

3 Make a 7" loopy bow with 10" streamers using sinamay ribbon. Glue on top of pine sprays. Glue one harvest pick in center of bow and one on each side of bow.

4 Make five 10" loop clusters by folding raffia in half. Wire ends to secure. Place raffia clusters in and around arrangement.

5 Fill in with dried-look statice.

6 Make nests for birds with Spanish moss. Glue two birds on pine sprays and one on top of house. Add small pieces of cedar sprays, nut sprays and statice. Glue in place.

7 For top of wreath, make same arrangement using smaller amounts of items. Glue birdhouse pick on top of wreath as shown.

Twenty nine

Rocking Horse Wreath

Materials:

- 1 - 24" Canadian Pine Wreath
- 1 - 9" Unfinished Rocking Horse
- 2 Stems - Gold Holly Spray
- 1 Stem - 20" Gold Plated Cedar Spray
- 3 Stems - Red Glittered Poinsettia
- 6 Yards - Red/Green Velvet Ribbon
- 1 Pkg. - Gold Glittered Birch Sticks
- Paint - Med. Brown, Red, Dk. Green, Black, White
- Brushes - #1 Liner, #4 Flat, #8 Flat
- Glue (hot glue recommended)

Instructions:

1 Paint rocking horse as follows: med. brown on horse's body, dk. green on rockers and inner saddle, red on bridle and outer saddle, black to fill in eye and white to highlight eye. When dry, glue horse into wreath facing left.

2 Cut one yard of ribbon for additional streamer, set aside. Make large, 10" loopy bow with 12" streamers. Glue to wreath at 4 o'clock position. Using one yard section of ribbon, weave in and out of pine branches in counter clockwise direction beginning at top of bow. Glue to secure.

3 Glue glittered gold birch sticks beneath loops of bow pointing in opposite directions, as shown. Fill in with gold holly and gold plated cedar spray.

4 Add red glitter poinsettias in graduated degrees of length. Refer to photograph for placement.

Thirty one

White Lily Wreath

Materials:

- 1 - 30" Canadian Pine Wreath
- 3 Stems - 18" Gold Plated Holly Spray
- 2 Stems - 20" White Plated Cedar Spray
- 12 Stems - Pearl White Berry Cluster
- 5 Stems - White Casablanca Lily
- 5 Yards - 2" Iridescent Wire Metallic Ribbon
- 1 Pkg. - Gold Glittered Birch Sticks
- Glue (hot glue recommended)

Instructions:

1 Glue gold glittered birch sticks on wreath at eleven o'clock position, pointing at an angle downwards, as shown.

2 Make a large florist bow 10" across with long streamers. Attach to wreath over birch sticks.

3 Cut lilies and glue as follows: twelve noon, two o'clock, ten o'clock, nine o'clock and six o'clock

4 Fill in with gold plated holly spray, white plated cedar pieces and frosted berries where needed. Refer to photograph for placement.